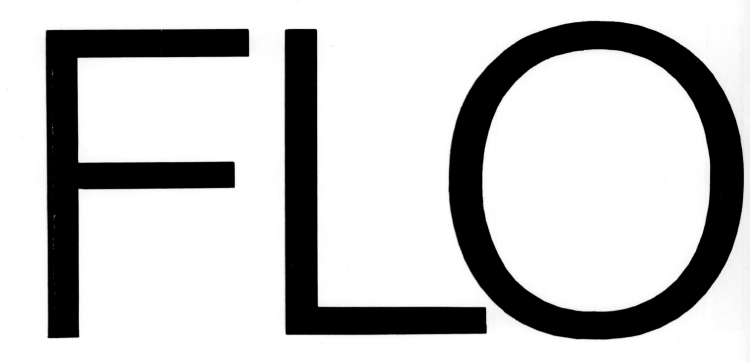

FLO

MIAMI AND MIAMI BEACH

EAST COAST

ATTRACTIONS

WEST COAST

THE EVERGLADES

KEY WEST

Published by Gallery Books
A Division of W H Smith Publishers Inc.
112 Madison Avenue
New York, New York 10016

Produced by
Bison Books Corporation
17 Sherwood Place
Greenwich, CT 06830

ISBN 0-8317-3391-8

Printed in Hong Kong
1 2 3 4 5 6 7 8 9 10

RIDA

PHOTOGRAPHY	MARCELLO BERTINETTI ANGELA WHITE BERTINETTI
TEXT	VALERIA MANFERTO DE FABIANIS
DESIGN	CARLO DE FABIANIS

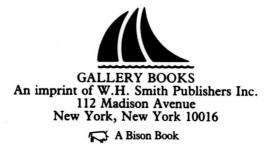

GALLERY BOOKS
An imprint of W.H. Smith Publishers Inc.
112 Madison Avenue
New York, New York 10016

A Bison Book

The authors wish to thank Gianna Manferto, Giorgio Tacchini, TWA and the Doral Hotel of Miami Beach for their cooperation.

The photographs taken at Walt Disney World and Epcot Center are printed by permission of Walt Disney Productions.

The photograph on page 81 is courtesy of NASA.

The photograph on pages 122-123 is by Gianni Lupari.

3/4/5/6 Cars and sailboats vie for parking space on Daytona Beach, one of the most famous and distinctive places in Florida.

Introduction

Soft, sunny beaches, luxurious hotels, a paradise of exotic wildlife, azure water beckoning lovers of deep-sea fishing — many experiences are available in Florida, all of which have made this state a Garden of Eden in the twentieth century. Yet less than 60 years ago, this part of America was almost unknown outside the United States. The rest of the world began to take an interest in 'the Sunshine State' only at the beginning of the Space Age, when the first American rockets took off from Cape Canaveral. But for many Americans from the northern states, the dream of Florida had always been there, as a goal at the end of their working life, the promise of a serene and quiet retirement in the warm southern sun, soothed by the ocean breezes.

The resourceful American spirit, and the people's firm sense of business and high professionalism, have changed this part of the country, adapting it to the wishes of its guests, creating an environment perfectly suited to relaxation. At present, Florida is the result of gigantic economic operations, which emphasize the deep contrasts between the more or less recent tourist attractions and the wilder aspects of the natural countryside. This includes such unique features as the wide marshes of the Everglades and the natural beauty of the offshore islands.

The history of Florida is, in many ways, like that of other American states: a history of exploration, colonization, battles for survival and independence. In other ways, however, it is completely different, especially for the period following the American Civil War.

The first Europeans to reach the coasts of Florida were the Spaniards, led by Don Juan Ponce de León who gave the new land its present name in 1513, inspired by a landfall on Easter, the Feast of Flowers (in Spanish, *Pascua Florida*). This inaugurated the period of Spanish colonization, which was soon followed by French and English incursions. The presence of so many foreign powers in the Caribbean caused many bloody battles, especially during the eighteenth century. After the Revolutionary Wars, the United States also began to show an interest in the territory, which was annexed in 1821. Florida became the 27th state in 1845, but seceded to join the Confederacy in 1861.

The real destiny of Florida began to be fulfilled after 1880. Two very rich and far-sighted men, Henry B Plant and Henry M Flagler, were the creators of modern Florida. At that time, Florida was still rather isolated from the rest of the United States: there were few interior roads, and the land was largely uninhabited. The main towns had fewer than 10,000 inhabitants, and Miami was a village with a few wooden huts.

Flagler and Plant built an efficient railway line which crossed the state — a feat achieved at great expense, and with no little difficulty. Then they began to build luxury hotels and tourist attractions along the two coasts. In 1885, Flagler opened his first hotel at St Augustine; ten years later, he began the development of Miami. In 1889, on the west coast, Plant began to build the Tampa Bay Hotel. By the end of the nineteenth century, Florida had acquired a reputation as one of the most exclusive resorts in the United States. In 1904, Flagler laid the foundation of his most ambitious plan: to join Key West to the rest of the state by railroad. Eight years later, it was completed. Today, Flagler's railroad has been supplanted by the Overseas Highway, which joins the chief keys by means of forty bridges and ends at Key West, less than 90 miles from the coast of Cuba.

Since 1920, Florida has continued to enjoy her transformation, becoming a popular place for vacations and rest. In the 1950s, it also became a symbol of progress, when the NASA space laboratories were established at Cape Canaveral. All these elements have brought incredible wealth and a growing population to the state. Florida's golden age continues, confirming the exceptional vision of Plant and Flagler.

Luxury houses and condominiums multiply, and big hotels are still being built to offer relaxing vacations to all types of guests. In Florida there is an atmosphere of serenity, jealously guarded from every external care.

In the 1960s, during the stormy years of confrontation over civil rights, Florida knew moments of great social tension: there were violent encounters among the different ethnic groups in many of the larger towns. Subsequently, public order was restored and tourism has increased again. As a result of some clever advertising, it continues even through the hot, wet summer season, creating jobs and increasing the flow of money.

The two coasts have experienced the same progress, but they have been able to create different attractions for different kinds of people. Such resorts as Palm Beach and Miami Beach on the east coast are the preserves of the very rich, businessmen and famous artists. On Daytona's hard-packed sands, thousands of lively students celebrate their spring breaks with weeks of partying. The west coast, especially around St Petersburg, has long been the ideal place for a quiet and serene retirement that allows for boating, fishing, golfing and other warm-weather activities.

Florida's appeal is due to a combination of natural features and man-made attractions, the varied activities it offers, its mild climate and the exciting atmosphere that prevails where a heterogeneous population is found. Traveling through the Everglades, it is possible to recapture the pioneer experience in a wild and primitive land. Several miles northward is the complex technology of Cape Canaveral, where man sets out to conquer space. Nearby, Walt Disney World allows people to wander through the charming fairy tales familiar to generations of children. In the shining corridors of EPCOT Center, one can visit an imagined future.

Florida, then, is a state where past and present, fantasy and reality coexist: a richly diverse land accepting of every aspect of man's search to make real even the most daring dream. Here it is possible to seek, and sometimes to find, the legendary treasures of the warm southern seas.

Valeria Manferto De Fabianis

Miami and Miami Beach

Miami, with Miami Beach, can be considered the prototype of the American tourist city. Here are all the elements that characterize American resorts: large hotels, skyscrapers, massive highways, amusement parks and, of course, the long white beaches and the warm and inviting ocean. The millionaires' houses hidden among the palm trees and lush gardens add a particularly luxurious atmosphere, which is heightened by the number of exclusive clubs. Because the population of Miami is so varied, it has become something unique — almost a Latin-American city in the United States. Many inhabitants are Cuban or Mexican; other Hispanics have come from Central or South America.

The city of Miami, which is now one of the greatest attractions in the United States, has a very recent history. In 1890, it had fewer than 1000 inhabitants; in 1896, the real expansion began, thanks to the railroad and hotels built by Henry M Flagler. Now it is one of the most populated and popular cities in the United States, with a wealth of unbelievable tourist attractions.

Actually there are two different cities: Miami, the commercial and financial center, and Miami Beach, the seaside and tourist resort. Geographically, they are separated by Biscayne Bay, but modern highways connect the two with six long causeways spanning the bay, which is dotted with artificial islands, covered with luxurious villas, complete with private piers and docks. Mass tourism has changed the flavor of these places, and the local inhabitants of Miami avoid the crowded sands of Miami Beach, preferring the more familiar and less commercial Key Biscayne.

These two components make Miami both one of the most important financial centers in the United States and one of the country's most frequented resorts. Much of the economic development of the city is due to the rich Cubans who settled here between 1959 and 1960, after the success of Fidel Castro's takeover in their own country. When they reached Miami, they bought available land and built many hotels and restaurants. In 'Little Havana' they have re-created the charming atmosphere of their own country, complete with sidewalk espresso stands.

Today, Miami continues to grow in a relaxing atmosphere where the small houses and markets of Little Havana develop in harmony with the luxury hotels of Miami Beach, accented by the lively colors of the beach umbrellas and the sails of the wind surfers.

14 The hotels of Miami Beach overlook Biscayne Bay and Miami Beach

15 Sunset reflections in the waters of Miami's Yacht Harbor. The city began as a settlement at the mouth of the Miami River in 1840, a minor harbor for ships sailing to the more important Key West.

16 Miami Beach is characterized by sparkling beaches and luxury hotels like the Doral, easily recognized by its slender tower.

17 The long shadows at sunset highlight the charm of an imaginative beach hut at Miami Beach.

18/19 An aerial view of Miami Beach, which is situated on the long barrier island east of Biscayne Bay and the city of Miami.

20/21 In Miami Harbor, the Caribbean cruise liners dock in the center of the city, at the feet of the skyscrapers.

22/23 The thick network of navigable canals on the southern outskirts of Miami allow owners of the luxurious houses in this area to moor their boats at home, an easy voyage from the open sea.

24 Miami International Airport is one of the
most important in the US for domestic flights
and those to Europe and South America

25 Jet-skiing has become a popular water
sport among young Floridians, who practice
during the weekends near Key Biscayne

26/27/28 The skyline of Miami from Treasure Island. Recently the city has developed extensively: it is now one of the financial centers of the nation.

29 Along the interior lagoon of Miami Beach, on Biscayne Bay, are the luxurious villas of the very rich. Spanish architectural style predominates, with red-tiled roofs and many porches and loggias.

30/31 Each hotel on Miami Beach has a distinctive color for its beach shelters and umbrellas. Together they make a colorful mosaic along the strand.

32/33 Colorful wind surfers skim along near Key Biscayne. This athletic sport is very popular among young Floridians.

34 top Business is transacted on the comfortable fantail of a yacht cruising the lagoon formed by Miami Beach.

34 bottom A drink on the terrace of the Doral Country Club, one of the most prestigious in the United States.

35 The greens and fairways of the Doral Country Club are world famous.

36/37 A private swimming pool and a perfect tan are within easy reach of many Florida residents.

38 The Cubans, who represent a sizeable
percentage of Miami's population, have
made an important contribution to the city's
economic and cultural development.

39 The residents of Little Havana congregate
in small cafes to play dominoes, just as they
did in Cuba.

40 *Spanish is the language of Little Havana,*
as seen in this coffee bar.

41 The night club Les Violins *specializes in
flamenco and Cuban entertainment that de-
lights both Spanish- and English-speaking
clientele.*

42/43 *The Art Deco district of Miami Beach
has many buildings in that distinctive style,
and a few other curiosities as well.*

East Coast

The east coast is that wonderful strip of beach which runs from Miami, in the southern part of the state, clear up to Jacksonville, near the border with Georgia, and contains some of the most famous and popular resorts in the Sunshine State.

North of Miami, the first town of importance is Fort Lauderdale. Known as the Venice of America, it is built on 165 miles of navigable canal. Its beach, lined with elegant hotels and bathing pavilions, offers hospitality to many rich patrons. The Fort Lauderdale harbor, at Port Everglades, contains modern marinas and is one of the chief ports for the liners on the Caribbean cruises.

Farther north is Palm Beach, which has been a favorite winter resort for many important American families since the 1920s. Luxurious mansions, private golf courses, swimming pools and large parks are still characteristic of Palm Beach, which can rightly be considered one of the most exclusive places in North America. It is easy to understand, why Worth Avenue has been called the 'Million Dollar Mile,' for its luxury shops which pack into only three city blocks the most famous names in international fashion.

A few miles above Cape Canaveral lie the Canaveral National Seashore and New Smyrna Beach, whose pristine shores offer hospitality to many exotic and rare birds, including the bald or American eagle. The increasingly scarce Florida manatee can also be sighted here.

Beyond Canaveral to the north is Daytona, famous for its long barrier beach and its very compact sand. In 1900, it became one of the first resorts in the state, renowned for the car races on the 20-mile-long beach. It was here, in 1903, that Alexander Winton broke the land speed record. Today, on this same beach, cars are still moving, but the speed limit is 10 minutes per hour. Like Fort Lauderdale, Daytona Beach is one of the meeting places for college students during spring break. The streets and beaches are filled with young people in bathing suits, and a cheerful party atmosphere envelops the entire town.

St Augustine, the oldest city in the United States, built in the mid sixteenth century, is different from the rest of Florida. The sense of history is almost tangible. Though two fires, in 1887 and 1914, have destroyed some of its most representative buildings, the ancient settlement still contains many glimpses of the past, especially in the design of its streets and lanes and in the remains of the Castillo de San Marcos, the fortress whose ramparts still confront those approaching by sea.

44 The compact sand of Daytona Beach allows cars to park close to the water.

45 Dawn breaking at New Smyrna Beach, one of the loveliest and least-known of the Florida resorts.

46 Worth Avenue in Palm Beach, where Mediterranean architecture sets off the famous shops selling the latest in luxury and fashion.

47 Fountains, tiles and flowering plants accent the courtyard shops behind Worth Avenue

48/49 *The clear skies and warm waters of*
Palm Beach attract visitors of all ages.

50/51 *The everyday wear of most Floridians . includes shorts and a beautiful tan.*

52 Brightly colored newspaper vending machines decorate a Palm Beach street.

53 In Fort Lauderdale, the residential areas are threaded by a thick network of canals, allowing boats to be moored just behind each house.

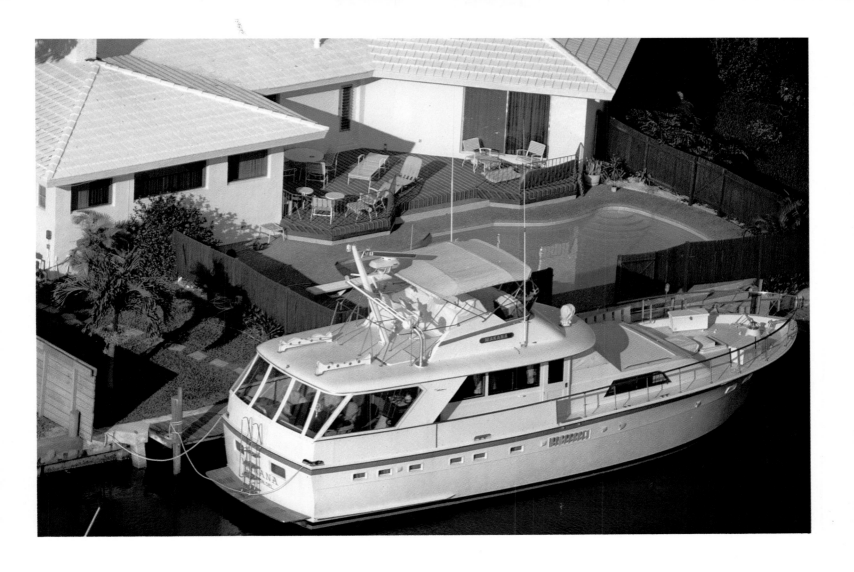

54/55 A view of Fort Lauderdale from the terrace of a top-floor restaurant.

56/57 The Canaveral National Seashore is an ideal place to enjoy the impressive spectacle of the sun rising out of the Atlantic Ocean.

58/59 The 20-mile-long beach at Daytona is a popular rendezvous for college students during spring break.

60/61 Ten miles per hour is the Daytona Beach speed limit. All sorts of vehicles can be seen cruising on the sand. Other people prefer to spend their time tanning along the water, or socializing over the roof of a car.

62 The ancient fortifications of Castillo de San Marcos still front the sea at St Augustine.

63 The city of St Augustine, the oldest in the United States, is now a popular tourist attraction.

Attractions

The remarkable and seemingly endless stream of tourists to Florida has created a number of attractions sustained by the amusement industry, which has developed in the United States as nowhere else.

Walt Disney Productions chose a large area near Orlando to build its most complex and complete fantasy park. Walt Disney World is one of the greatest urban centers born solely of private enterprise. Begun in 1967, it required enormous land reclamation efforts. Thousands worked relentlessly, modifying the topography of Central Florida, creating artificial hills and lakes, building hotels and restaurants, as well as the extraordinary structures that make up the amusement park itself. The core of all this is the Magic Kingdom, where the characters created by the magical mind of Walt Disney circulate among the crowds with a friendly smile for everyone. Near this kingdom of fantasy is EPCOT, the Experimental Prototype Community of Tommorrow. This world of the future was created in collaboration with the scientists and technicians of the Kennedy Space Center.

Among the attractions of Florida are many that take full advantage of the climate and local fauna. At Sea World, for instance, near Orlando, trained killer whales and dolphins perform. At Cypress Gardens there is a remarkable waterskiing show in a lush and exotic garden. At the amusement park called Wet n' Wild, an incredible series of giant slides, water flumes, artificial waves and swimming pools offers the visitor a damp and amusing afternoon. At Weeki Wachee Springs, charming mermaids perform in a unique under-water spectacle.

Some visitors feel that no amusement park can compete with the thrills afforded by the Kennedy Space Center. Here, among the rockets that made flights to the moon, the visitor can experience simulated flight in pressurized cabins and enter the vast hangers that house the enormous rockets. Every year Cape Canaveral is visited by thousands of people, who pay tribute to NASA's great achievements.

64 The visitor to the Kennedy Space Center is greeted by a line of rocket prototypes used in the NASA space program.

65 Cinderella's Castle, the symbol of Walt Disney World, rises over the huge complex visited by millions each year.

66/67 Walt Disney's characters, Mickey and Minnie Mouse, greet visitors to Walt Disney World.

68/69 A spectacular fireworks display lights the sky during the tenth anniversary celebration of Walt Disney World

70 EPCOT Center, which opened in 1982, is
the fulfillment of Walt Disney's last dream: to
show life in the future through the wonder of
sophisticated technology.

71 The entrance to EPCOT is dominated by
Spaceship Earth, a geodesic dome housing
an exhibit that allows the visitor to walk
through the history of mankind.

72/73 Florida is an ideal place for a family vacation because of the many attractions directed at children.

74/75 At Sea World, near Orlando, water-skiers perform in an acrobatic display.

76 At the big Sea World Aquarium, Shamu, the famous killer whale, performs each day in an aquatic show that also features porpoises, dolphins and seals.

77 In the clear waters of Weeki Wachee Springs, 'mermaids' perform in a water show viewed through a panoramic glass window 16 feet below the surface.

78 top At Circus World, near Orlando, clowns perform daily.

78 bottom A hangglider soaring over Cypress Gardens.

79 The water slide at Wet n'Wild is one of the attractions that lets the visitor cool off in the Florida heat.

82/83 Near Lake Okeechobee, traditional cattle auctions continue to play an important part in the lives of Florida ranchers.

80 A mighty Saturn rocket on display at the Kennedy Space Center.

81 A rocket launched from the Kennedy Space Center can be seen from the nearby Canaveral National Seashore.

West Coast

The west coast is the preferred vacation spot for those looking for rest in a quiet and relaxing atmosphere. The center of this coast is Tampa, and the nearby towns of St Petersburg and Sarasota. The rest of the coast is still quite underdeveloped, despite the number of tourist attractions, designed to compete with the well-known sites on the east coast, which are now under construction. This is the case with Marco Island near Naples, which is fast becoming one of the best-known resorts on the Gulf of Mexico.

In the last few years, Tampa, with its lovely natural harbor, has undergone remarkable development. This may be quite suprising if one is expecting a typical seaside resort with rustling palm trees, or the holiday atmosphere of Miami Beach or Key West. On the contrary, the city is a modern American metroplis growing larger and larger, and one of the most important commercial centers in the country. The high burnished-glass sky-scrapers mirroring the heavy traffic of the main urban streets, and the big department stores where people are always in a hurry, are as typical of Tampa as of any other modern mercantile center. Side by side are rapid commercial growth and a resort of rare beauty, where nothing is lacking for relaxation and amusement.

There are two more tourist centers on the west coast: across Tampa Bay lies St Petersburg, called the Sun City, famous for its particularly healthy climate; to the south is Sarasota, which is often compared with the more famous Palm Beach for its discreet and refined appearance. It is an important cultural center and offers hospitality to artists and writers. Its theater, the Asolo, presents classical and modern drama. However, the most typical image of the west coast is still that of long virgin beaches where pelicans and sea gulls dive into the waters of the Gulf of Mexico in the warm sunset light.

84 The skyline of Tampa, the growing commercial center of Florida's Gulf Coast.

85 The white beach of St. Petersburg, on the Gulf of Mexico is one of the most beautiful in Florida.

86/87 The pristine sand is emphasized by the brightly colored shelters that dot the beach at St Petersburg.

88 The harbor at Tampa is a major port for
luxury liners and freighters from South
America and the Bahamas.

89 The downtown area of Tampa, over-
looking the bay, is in a constant state of
construction, as many businesses move
south to enjoy the climate.

90/91 The glass skyscrapers of Tampa reflect the ever-changing clouds and the perfect blue of the Florida sky.

92/93 Bathers at Madeira Beach take a last swim at twilight.

94 The Gulf Coast is famous for the number and variety of seabirds that flock there.

95 The pelican, with its curious bill, has become a symbol of this part of Florida.

Everglades

The region of the Everglades, at the southern tip of Florida, begins as a series of grassy, low-lying meadows which give way to vast mangrove swamps. The Everglades National Park, at 1,400,000 acres the third largest in the United States, covers only the southwest part of this area.

Until 1915, this diverse wilderness, known only to hunters, Seminole Indians and explorers, was considered dangerous and unfit for human habitation. With the passing of time, however, this land rich in legend aroused curiosity. Owing to the rare flora and fauna, it was included in the nature and preservation plan which, in 1947, gave rise to the Everglades National Park. An efficient system of control and a staff of skillful and qualified rangers protect the land and encourage the survival of many species. At the same time, tourists are permitted to visit this unspoiled habitat.

Presently the Everglades National Park is home to more than 300 species of birds, some of which seemed doomed to extinction until recently. In the most remote parts are found panthers, black bears, otters, raccoons, wildcats, deer and alligators. All of these and more can be found in one of the most spectacular and distinct environments in the whole world: an endless sea of grass and reeds waving in the warm evening breezes, or swaying madly in the hurricanes that ravage this area with awesome force during the summer and early fall.

A palette of infinite golden hues, the grass is dazzling when the sun shines. Toward sunset, by comparison, everything turns red and becomes an indefinite, rustling mass in the encroaching darkness. Before a storm, the sky is full of low and dark clouds quickly passing by, and the strengthening wind bends and often destroys all that stands in its way. The rains come on violently, and the air is filled with strange noises—frogs and insects. Suddenly all is still, and the sun pierces through the clouds, and, as if by magic, a rainbow appears. The animals, which at first sign of the storm had fled into their dens, return, and the thousands of birds resume their chattering.

All these adventures can now be experienced by man safely, thanks to the organization of the park. From Flamingo, a small village in the southern end of the Everglades, it is possible to hire boats to visit the innermost parts of the park where the vegetation is most luxuriant, or to reach the Gulf of Mexico, where reeds and grasses give way to the intricate roots of the mangroves.

96 Twisted mangrove roots break the water's surface in Everglades National Park.

97 A pelican diving in the warm water of Florida Bay.

98 The peaceful harbor at Flamingo, one of the tourist centers in the Everglades.

99 Among the residents of the Everglades are guides who can steer the visitor through the tangle of swamps and waterways.

100/101 The double rainbow after a storm illuminates the grass meadows of the northern Everglades.

102/103 Ominous dark clouds presage a tropical storm over the Everglades National Park.

104/105 *The American alligator is perhaps
the most famous resident of the Everglades.
Many visitors make the long trip to Florida in
the hope of sighting this giant reptile.*

106 *The curious roots of the mangrove
spread through the dark water of the
Everglades.*

107 A turtle plays hide-and-seek among the water lilies in the Everglades.

108/109 The great blue heron, magnificent in flight, is one of the rare birds found in Everglades National Park.

Key West

The sun going down below the horizon creates a wonderful tropical sunset; the pink hues deepen and sharply mark the outlines of the low wooden houses and the flowering trees. Each evening in Key West, people gather near the harbor, as if by invitation. An acrobat on a tightrope stretched over the water performs for the crowd below, whirling flaming torches which seem to echo the last rays of the setting sun. Gradually the evening turns to the deep velvet tropical night, but in Key West the streets do not empty. On the contrary, the island becomes more vibrant.

The lively nightlife ends only at dawn, when once again the slow, lazy rhythm of the day returns. This is typical of Key West, which though joined to mainland Florida by the Overseas Highway has preserved a peculiar flavor all its own.

In the past, the island was a lair of pirates and wreckers who had a thriving market in treasures from the ships lost on the dangerous reefs. Later it became the center for turtle fishing and sponge gathering. In the second half of the nineteenth century, it became rich, thanks to a tobacco industry undertaken to compete which that of Cuba. This halcyon period ended abruptly in 1929, when the Wall Street crash shocked all America.

Key West was especially hard hit by the economic and social consequences of this period, and most of its inhabitants left to live on the mainland. In the 1930s, the situation began to improve, as the developing tourist industry brought money back into the area. In a short time, new buildings, the restoration of the historical center, the tropical climate, the deep-water fishing became a tremendous pull. Key West offered hospitality to many famous people, including President Harry S Truman, and to writers and artists looking for peace and inspiration. The man who is best known in connection with the island is undoubtedly Ernest Hemingway, who lived there for 12 years with his family. His strong personality can still be felt on the piers, in the garden of his house, now a museum, and above all, in the rooms of Sloppy Joe's, his favorite bar and hangout. Here he wrote some of his most famous novels: *A Farewell to Arms*, *Death in the Afternoon* and *The Green Hills of Africa*.

With the passing of time, in spite of inevitable changes, Key West has been able to preserve the traces of the past. It has once again grown rich through the happy experiences of all those who have been lucky enough to live there for a while.

110 Elaborate ironwork and flags decorate Key West facades.

111 An acrobat, silhouetted against the setting sun, entertains at the evening festivities at Key West Harbor.

112/113 An aerial view of Key West: a town of historic and strategic importance, it has become a popular tourist resort.

114/115 The Overseas Highway, running parallel to Flagler's railroad, links the Florida Keys. Seven Mile Bridge, built on a barrier reef, joins Piscon Key to Bahia Honda Key.

116 The streets of Key West, despite the popularity of the town, retain an informal charm that makes bike-riding a pleasure.

117 Captain Tony's Saloon was once Sloppy Joe's Bar, a frequent haunt of the writer Ernest Hemingway.

118 Hemingway's house, now a museum, is built in the Spanish Colonial style typical of Key West.

119/120 Contentment and pleasure are emotions felt by every visitor to Key West.

121 Treasure hunter Mel Fisher displays some of the gold recovered from the Spanish galleon Nuestra Señora de Atocha, which sank in 1622.

122/123 The barrier reef and warm tropical waters are home to many species of exotic and brightly colored fish.

124/125 Nowhere is sunset more dramatic than at Key West, as the sun sinks into the warm tropical water of the Gulf of Mexico.

126 Sand Key, not far from Key West, is a popular rendezvous for tourists who explore the keys by boat.